BRINGING COMMUNION TO THE SICK

A Handbook for Ministers of Holy Communion

BRINGING COMMUNION TO THE SICK

A Handbook for Ministers of Holy Communion

VERITAS

Published 2012 by
Veritas Publications
7–8 Lower Abbey Street, Dublin 1, Ireland
publications@veritas.ie
www.veritas.ie

ISBN 978 1 84730 371 4

10 9 8 7 6

Imprimatur: ✠ Diarmuid Martin, Archbishop of Dublin

Typesetting: Colette Dower, Veritas Publications
Printed in the Republic of Ireland by Paceprint Ltd, Dublin

Contents

Introduction

The sick or aged, even though not seriously ill or in danger of death, should be given every opportunity to receive the Eucharist frequently, even daily, especially during the Easter season.

They may receive Holy Communion, at any hour. Those who care for the sick may receive Holy Communion with them. Neither the elderly and the sick, nor those who care for them, are bound to the eucharistic fast of one hour.

The priest and deacon are the ordinary ministers of Holy Communion. Men and women, duly appointed as ministers are called extraordinary ministers of Holy Communion.

Each community should ensure that there is a sufficient number of ministers to provide frequent Holy Communion for the sick.

Those who are ill, and the elderly who are housebound, are deprived of their rightful and accustomed place in the eucharistic community. In bringing Holy Communion to them, the minister of Holy Communion represents Christ and manifests faith and charity on behalf of the whole community towards those who cannot be present at Mass. For the sick the reception of Holy Communion is not only a privilege but also a sign of support and concern shown by the Christian community for its members who are ill.

The community at Mass, especially on Sundays, is linked in a special way with the sick who receive Holy

Communion. The community remembers the sick in the Universal Prayer or the Prayer of the Faithful, and should be reminded occasionally of the significance of Holy Communion in the lives of those who are ill: union with Christ in his struggle with evil, his prayer for the world, and his love for the Father, and union with the community from which they are separated.

This symbol of unity between the community and its sick members has the deepest significance on Sunday, the special day of the eucharistic assembly. The minister can help the sick person to share in that day's Liturgy of the Word, by using the proper readings and recalling the words of the celebrant's homily.

Those who are with the sick should be shown how to prepare a table covered with a linen cloth upon which the blessed sacrament will be placed. Lighted candles are prepared. Care should be taken to make the occasion special and joyful. The sick person may help to plan the celebration by choosing prayers and readings. In making these choices the condition of the sick person should be kept in mind.

Sick people who are unable to receive Holy Communion under the form of bread may receive it under the form of wine alone.

Priests should make regular visits to the sick and aged since they may wish to celebrate the Sacrament of Penance.

The Ordinary Rite of Holy Communion of the Sick

Introductory Rites

The minister greets the sick person and the others present in a friendly manner. This greeting may be used:

Peace to this house and all who live in it.

Any other customary greeting from scripture may be used. Then the minister places the Blessed Sacrament on the table and all adore it.

The minister invites the sick person and those present to recall their sins and to repent of them in these words:

**My brothers and sisters,
let us acknowledge our sins,
and so prepare ourselves for this celebration.**

A pause for silent reflection follows, then the rite continues using one of the following:

A

I confess to almighty God
and to you, my brothers and sisters,
that I have greatly sinned,
in my thoughts and in my words,
in what I have done and in what I have failed to
do,

And, striking their breast, they say:

through my fault, through my fault,
through my most grievous fault;

Then they continue:

therefore I ask blessed Mary ever-Virgin,
all the Angels and Saints,
and you, my brothers and sisters,
to pray for me to the Lord our God.

Or

B

The minister:

Have mercy on us, O Lord.

The people reply:

For we have sinned against you.

The Priest:

Show us, O Lord, your mercy.

The people:

And grant us your salvation.

Or

C

The minister:

Lord Jesus, you healed the sick:
Lord, have mercy.

The people reply:

Lord, have mercy.

The minister:

Lord Jesus, you forgave sinners:
Christ, have mercy.

The people:

Christ, have mercy.

The minister:

Lord Jesus, you give us yourself to heal us
and bring us strength:
Lord, have mercy.

The people:

Lord, have mercy.

_____

The minister:

May almighty God have mercy on us,
forgive us our sins,
and bring us to everlasting life.

The people reply:

Amen.

The Short Form of the Reading of the Word

A brief passage from sacred scripture may then be read by one of those present or by the minister.

A
John 6:51

Jesus says:
'I am the living bread which has come down from heaven.
Anyone who eats this bread will live for ever;
and the bread that I shall give
is my flesh, for the life of the world.'

B
John 6:54-58

Jesus says:
'Anyone who eats my flesh and drinks my blood
has eternal life,
and I shall raise him up on the last day.
For my flesh is real food
and my blood is real drink.
He who eats my flesh and drinks my blood
lives in me
and I live in him.
As I, who am sent by the living Father,
myself draw life from the Father,
so whoever eats me will draw life from me.
This is the bread come down from heaven;
not like the bread our ancestors ate:
they are dead,
but anyone who eats this bread will live for ever.'

C
John 14:6

Jesus says:
'I am the Way, the Truth and the Life.
No one can come to the Father except through me.'

D
John 15:5

Jesus says:
'I am the vine, you are the branches.
Whoever remains in me, with me in him,
bears fruit in plenty;
for cut off from me you can do nothing.'

E
John 15:4

Jesus says:
'Make your home in me, as I make mine in you.
As a branch cannot bear fruit all by itself, but
must remain part of the vine,
neither can you unless you remain in me.'

F
John 14:27

Jesus says:
'Peace I bequeath to you,
my own peace I give you,
a peace the world cannot give, this is my gift to
you.
Do not let your hearts be troubled or afraid.'

G
John 4:16

We ourselves have known and put our faith in
God's love towards ourselves.
God is love
and anyone who lives in love lives in God,
and God lives in him.

H
Matthew 11:25-30

Jesus exclaimed:
I bless you, Father, Lord of heaven and of earth,
for hiding these things from the learned and the
clever and revealing them to mere children.
Yes, Father, for that is what it pleased you to do.
Everything has been entrusted to me by my
Father and no one knows the Son except the
Father,
just as no one knows the Father except the Son
and those to whom the Son chooses to reveal him.
Come to me, all you who labour and are
overburdened,
and I will give you rest.
Shoulder my yoke and learn from me,
for I am gentle and humble in heart,
and you will find rest for your souls.
Yes, my yoke is easy and my burden light.

Other Readings from Sacred Scripture, pp. 22-26.

Holy Communion

The minister then introduces the Lord's Prayer in these or similar words:

**At the Saviour's command
and formed by divine teaching,
we dare to say:**

Our Father, who art in heaven,
hallowed be thy name;
thy kingdom come,
thy will be done
on earth as it is in heaven.
Give us this day our daily bread,
and forgive us our trespasses,
as we forgive those who trespass against us;
and lead us not into temptation,
but deliver us from evil.

Then the minister shows the Holy Eucharist to those present, saying:

**Behold the Lamb of God,
behold him who takes away the sins of the
world.**

Blessed are those called to the supper of the Lamb.

The sick person and the other communicants say:

Lord, I am not worthy
that you should enter under my roof,
but only say the word
and my soul shall be healed.

The minister goes to the sick person. Raising the host slightly, the minister shows it to the communicant, saying:

The Body of Christ (or: **The Blood of Christ**)

The sick person answers:

Amen.

and received Holy Communion.

Others present who wish to receive communion then do so in the usual way.

After the conclusion of the rite, the minister cleanses the vessel as usual.

Then a period of silence may be observed.

The minister says a concluding prayer. One of the
following may be used.

Let us pray.

A

All-powerful and ever-living God,
may the body and blood of Christ your Son
be for our brother/sister N.
a lasting remedy for body and soul.
Through Christ our Lord.
Amen.

Or

B

God our Father,
you have called us to share the one bread and
one cup
and so become one in Christ.
Help us to live in him
that we may bear fruit,
rejoicing that he has redeemed the world.
Through Christ our Lord.
Amen.

Or

C

All powerful God,
we thank you for the nourishment you give us
through your holy gift.
Pour out your Spirit upon us
and in the strength of this food from heaven
keep us singleminded in your service.
Through Christ our Lord.
Amen.

Or

D

Father,
you have brought to fulfilment the work of
our redemption
through the easter mystery of Christ your
Son.
May we who faithfully proclaim his death
and resurrection
in these sacramental signs
experience the constant growth of your
salvation in our lives.
Through Christ our Lord.
Amen.

Concluding Rite

Then the minister invokes God's blessing, making the sign of the cross on himself or herself, while saying:

A

May the Lord bless us,
protect us from all evil,
and bring us to everlasting life.
Amen.

Or

B

May the almighty and merciful God bless
and protect us,
the Father, and the Son, and the Holy Spirit.
Amen.

When Holy Communion is given in different rooms of the same building, such as a hospital, a shorter rite is to be used. It may begin in the church or chapel or in the first room, where the minister says an antiphon or prayer or reads a short passage from Sacred Scripture. The minister says to all the sick persons in the same room or to each communicant individually the invitation to Holy Communion: Behold the Lamb of God … Holy Communion is received in the usual manner. The rite is concluded with a prayer which may be said in the church or chapel or in the last room. Elements taken from the Ordinary Rite may be added according to circumstances.

Other Readings from Sacred Scripture

1
1 Kings 19:2-8

Elijah was afraid and fled for his life. He came to
Beersheba, a town of Judah, where he left his
servant. He himself went on into the wilderness, a
day's journey; and sitting under a furze bush
wished he were dead. 'Lord,' he said, 'I have had
enough. Take my life; I am no better than my
ancestors.' Then he lay down and went to sleep.
But an angel touched him and said, 'Get up and
eat'. He looked round, and there at his head was a
scone baked on hot stones, and a jar of water. He
ate and drank and then lay down again. But the
angel of the Lord came back a second time and
touched him and said, 'Get up and eat,or the
journey will be too long for you.' So he got up and
ate and drank, and strengthened by that food he
walked for forty days and forty nights until he
reached Horeb, the mountain of God.

2
Psalm 62

Response: For you my soul is thirsting, O God my God.

O God, you are my God, for you I long;
for you my soul is thirsting.
My body pines for you
like a dry weary land without water.
So I gaze on you in the sanctuary
to see your strength and your glory. R.

For your love is better than life,
my lips will speak your praise.
So I will bless you all my life,
in your name I will lift up my hands.
My soul shall be filled as with a banquet,
my mouth shall praise you with joy. R.

On my bed I remember you.
On you I muse through the night
for you have been my help;
in the shadow of your wings I rejoice.
My soul clings to you;
your right hand holds me fast. R.

3
2 Corinthians 4:16-18

There is inner renewal day by day.
There is no weakening on our part, and instead,
though this outer man of ours may be falling into
decay,
the inner man is renewed day by day.
Yes, the troubles which are soon over,
though they weigh little,
train us for the carrying of a weight of eternal
glory
which is out of all proportion to them.
And so we have no eyes for things that are visible,
but only for things that are invisible;
for visible things last only for a time,
and the invisible things are eternal.

4
Psalm 22

Response: If I should walk in the valley of darkness no evil would I fear.

The Lord is my shepherd;
there is nothing I shall want.
Fresh and green are the pastures
where he gives me repose.
Near restful waters he leads me,
to revive my drooping spirit. R.

He guides me along the right path;
he is true to his name.
If I should walk in the valley of darkness
no evil would I fear.
You are there with your crook and your staff;
with these you give me comfort. R.

You have prepared a banquet for me
in the sight of my foes.
My head you have anointed with oil;
my cup is overflowing. R.

Surely goodness and kindness shall follow me
all the days of my life.
In the Lord's own house shall I dwell
for ever and ever. R.

5
Matthew 8:14-7

Going into Peter's house Jesus found Peter's
mother-in-law in bed with fever. He touched her
hand and the fever left her, and she got up and
began to wait on him.

That evening they brought him many who were
possessed by devils. He cast out the spirits with a
word and cured all who were sick. This was to
fulfil the prophecy of Isaiah:

He took our sicknesses away
and carried our diseases for us.

Short Devotional Prayers

Some of the following prayers may be said with the sick person by the minister of the eucharist.

From the Psalms

O Lord, listen to my prayer and let my cry for help reach you. *(101:2)*

Let us see, O Lord, your mercy, and give us your saving help. *(84:8)*

Let your face shine on us, O Lord, and we shall be saved. *(79:4)*

Our eyes are on the Lord till he shows us his mercy. *(122:3)*

Have mercy on us, O Lord, have mercy. *(122:4)*

I thank you, Lord, for your faithfulness and love. *(137:2)*

May the name of the Lord be blessed for evermore! *(112:2)*

O God, do not treat us according to our sins. *(102:10)*

Have mercy on us, O Lord, for we have sinned. *(50:3)*

If you, O Lord, should mark our guilt, Lord who would survive? *(129:3)*

Into your hands I commend my spirit, O Lord. *(30:6)*

Give thanks to the Lord for he is good, for his love has no end. *(117:1)*

In your great love, answer me, O Lord. *(68:21)*

The Lord is my shepherd; there is nothing I shall want. *(22:1)*

Here I am, Lord, I come to do your will. *(33:8.9)*

May the name of the Lord be blessed for evermore. *(112:2)*

The Lord fills the earth with his love. *(32:5)*

Remember your mercy, Lord. *(24:6)*

The love of the Lord is everlasting upon those who hold him in fear. *(102:17)*

O Lord, I trust in your merciful love. *(12:6)*

Turn to me, Lord, and have mercy. *(24:16)*

Lord, forgive the wrong I have done. *(31:5)*

Fill us with your love, O Lord, and we shall rejoice. *(89:14)*

Teach me to do your will, my God. *(142:10)*

Have mercy on me, Lord, I have no strength. *(6:3)*

God of mercy and compassion, turn and take pity on me. *(85:15.16)*

The Lord is close to the broken-hearted. *(33:9)*
My God, make haste to help me. *(70:12)*
To you, O Lord, I lift up my soul. *(24:16)*
The Lord is compassion and love, slow to anger
and rich in mercy. *(102:1)*

Blessed are they who put their trust in God. *(2:13)*
Do not abandon or forsake me, O God my help.
(26:9)

Other Prayers

Lord Jesus, you are the Christ, the Son of the
living God.
Lord Jesus, you are the Resurrection and the Life.
Lord Jesus, we believe in you.

 Lord Jesus, we adore you.

Lord Jesus, you are the Bread of Life.

 Lord Jesus, we hope in you.

Lord, the one whom you love is sick.

 Lord, say but the word and I shall be healed.

Lord, that I may see.

 Lord, increase our faith.

Lord, lead us in your ways.

 Lord, take away my selfishness.

Jesus, Son of David, have pity on us.

> Lord, save us for we perish.

Lord, without you we can do nothing.

> Lord, give your peace to the world.

Lord, have pity on your starving people.

> Lord, help us to work for peace.

Lord, teach us to love.

> Lord, increase our love.

Lord, increase the holiness of your Church.

> Lord, make us one in love.

Lord, I believe, help my unbelief.

> Glory and praise to you, Lord Jesus Christ.

My soul glorifies the Lord, my spirit rejoices in God my Saviour.

He looks on his servant in her lowliness, henceforth all ages will call me blessed.

The Almighty works marvels for me, holy is His name.

His mercy is from age to age, on those who fear Him.

He puts forth His arm in strength, and scatters the proudhearted.

He casts the mighty from their thrones, and raises the lowly.

He fills the starving with good things, sends the rich away empty.
He protects Israel his servant remembering his mercy,
the mercy promised to our fathers, to Abraham and his sons for ever.

Prayers for the Minister

Before visiting the sick
Lord, send your Holy Spirit to work within me
and through me.
Let the words I use be a source of comfort and
strength to those I care for;
and may you be glorified through Jesus Christ our
Lord. Amen.

Lord Jesus Christ, filled with the Spirit, you
brought the good news to
the poor and relieved the distress of the sick and
sorrowful.
Be with me in this ministry
that I also may, in humility and love,
be a comfort and help to those in need. Amen.

Lord Jesus, our Saviour, you have compassion for
all the sick and infirm:
be with me as I bring your saving presence to our
brothers and sisters.

Fill them with new life; give them strength and hope;
be to them a pledge of everlasting life. Amen.

Some reflections for the Minister

A

If one member suffers in the Body of Christ, which is the Church, all the members suffer with that member. (1 Cor 12:26). For this reason, kindness shown towards the sick, and works of charity and mutual help for the relief of every kind of human want are held in special honour.

It is thus especially fitting that all baptised Christians share in this ministry of mutual charity within the Body of Christ by doing all that they can to help the sick return to health, by showing love for the sick, and celebrating the sacraments with them.

The family and friends of the sick and those who take care of them in any way have a special share in this ministry of comfort. In particular, it is their task to strengthen the sick with words of faith and by praying with them, to commend them to the

suffering and glorified Lord, and to encourage them to contribute to the well-being of the people of God by associating themselves willingly with Christ's passion and death.
Pastoral Care of the Sick. *nos. 32-34, (Veritas Publications, 1983)*

B

The minister to whom this visitation of the sick is a routine duty to be performed because it is expected of him; who is depressed himself by what he sees; who is not conscious of any divine mission and does not expect to accomplish any divine results, knows nothing of the possibilities that lie before him. But the one who enters this realm of suffering deeply aware of his great privilege and opportunity, who is filled with the spirit of reverence at what he finds there, who equips himself with all the resources at his command and exercises his calling with all the care and skill that knowledge of both God and man can give him, can repeat the miracles of grace of Him to whom no sufferer ever looked in vain.
Raymond Calkins (From F. B. MacNutt, The Prayer Manuals, *Mowbray, London 1951)*

C

Jesus' ministry to the sick is continued in his Body, the Church, itself a sign and instrument of the kingdom, a leaven among the nations. The Good Samaritan is the model of Christian compassion towards our suffering brothers and sisters. Jesus goes so far as to identify himself with the sick: 'I was sick and you visited me.'

Jesus promised to be present to us 'always, to the close of the age'. His is a reconciling presence, a ministry of reconciliation entrusted to his Church. The Church's mission in the world is to be a loving, healing, reconciling presence with special concern and affection for the helpless, the sick, the infirm, and the aging.

Reflecting the attitude of its founder, the Church's option should always be first of all for the poor and lowly. This overall ministry of reconciliation and healing exerts a prophetic and humanising influence on social and environmental issues so easily overlooked …

The Church's ministry of healing should not be isolated or viewed apart from the rest of its mission to be a visible sign of Christ's continued presence in the world.

Charles W Gusmer (From And you visited me, *Pueblo Publishing Co., New York, 1984)*

D

As Veronica ministered to Christ on his way to Calvary, so Christians have accepted the care of those in pain and sorrow as privileged opportunities to minister to Christ himself.
Remember it is Christ to whom you minister in the sufferings of your brothers and sisters.
Do not neglect your sick and elderly.
Do not turn away from the handicapped and dying.
Do not push them to the margins of society.
For if you do, you will fail to understand that they represent an important truth.
The sick, the elderly, the handicapped, and the dying teach us that weakness is a creative part of human living, and that suffering can be embraced with no loss of dignity.

Without the presence of these people in your midst you might be tempted to think of health, strength, and power as the only important values to be pursued in life.

But the wisdom of Christ and the power of Christ are to be seen in the weakness of those who share his sufferings.

Let us keep the sick and the handicapped at the centre of our lives.

Let us treasure them and recognise with gratitude the debt we owe them.

We begin by imagining that we are giving to them; we end by realising that they have enriched us.

Pope John Paul II (From his homily in St George's Southwark, London, 28 May 1982, CTS, London)

E

Christians, especially ministers, so often think they must always contribute something when they are in the company of others, that this is the one service they have to render. They forget that listening can be a greater service than speaking.

Many people are looking for an ear that will listen. They do not find it among Christians, because these Christians are talking when they should be listening. But they who can no longer listen to their brothers and sisters will soon be no longer listening to God either; they will be doing nothing but prattle in the presence of God too.

Dietrich Bonhoeffer (From Life together, *trs. J. W. Doberstein, New York, Harper, 1954.)*

Celebration of Viaticum

The celebration of the Eucharist as Viaticum, food for the passage through death to eternal life, is the sacrament proper to the dying Christian. It is the completion and crown of the Christian life on this earth, signifying that the Christian follows the Lord to eternal glory and the banquet of the heavenly kingdom.

All entrusted with the spiritual care of the sick should do everything that they can to ensure that those in proximate danger of death receive the Body and Blood of Christ as Viaticum.

Whenever it is possible, the dying Christian should be able to receive Viaticum within Mass.

However, circumstances may sometimes make the complete eucharistic celebration impossible and allow for the Rite for Viaticum outside Mass to be celebrated by an extraordinary minister of Holy Communion.

The Rite of Viaticum

Introductory Rites

The minister greets the sick person and the others present in a friendly manner. This greeting may be used:

Peace to this house and all who live in it.

Any other customary greeting from scripture may be used. Then he places the Blessed Sacrament on the table and all adore it.

The minister addresses those present, using the following instruction or one better suited to the sick person's condition.

My brothers and sisters, before our Lord Jesus Christ passed from this world to return to the Father, he left us the Sacrament of his Body and Blood. When the hour comes for us to pass from this life and join him, he strengthens us with this food for our journey and comforts us by this pledge of our resurrection.

The minister invites the sick person and those present to recall their sins and to repent of them in these words:

My brothers and sisters,
let us acknowledge our sins,
and so prepare ourselves for this celebration.

A pause for silent reflection follows.

A

All say:

I confess to almighty God
and to you, my brothers and sisters,
that I have greatly sinned,
in my thoughts and in my words,
in what I have done and in what I have failed to do,

And, striking their breast, they say:

through my fault, through my fault,
through my most grievous fault;

Then they continue:

therefore I ask blessed Mary, ever-Virgin,
all the Angels and Saints,
and you, my brothers and sisters,
to pray for me to the Lord our God.

B

The minister says:

By your paschal mystery you have won for us salvation: Lord, have mercy.

The people reply:

Lord, have mercy.

The minister says:

You renew us by the wonders of your passion: Christ, have mercy.

The people reply:

Christ, have mercy.

The minister says:

You give us your body to make us one with your Paschal sacrifice: Lord, have mercy

The people reply:

Lord, have mercy.

The minister concludes:

May almighty God have mercy on us, forgive us our sins, and bring us to everlasting life.

The people reply:

Amen.

The Short Form of the Reading of the Word

A brief passage from sacred scripture may then be read by one of those present or by the minister.

A
John 6:54-55

Jesus says:
Anyone who eats my flesh and drinks my blood
has eternal life,
and I shall raise him up on the last day.
for my flesh is real food
and my blood is real drink.

The Gospel of the Lord.

B
John 14:23

Jesus says:
If anyone loves me he will keep my word,
and my Father will love him,
and we shall come to him
and make our home with him.

The Gospel of the Lord.

C
John 15:4

Jesus says:
Make your home in me, as I make mine in you.
As a branch cannot bear fruit all by itself,
but must remain part of the vine,
neither can you unless you remain in me.

D
1 Corinthians 11:26

Until the Lord comes, therefore, every time you
eat this bread and drink this cup, you are
proclaiming his death.

Profession of Baptismal Faith

It is desirable that the sick person renew his or her baptismal
profession of faith before viaticum. The minister gives a
brief introduction and then asks the following questions:

**N. do you believe in God, the Father
Almighty, creator of heaven and earth?**

The sick person and those present reply:
I do.

The minister continues:

Do you believe in Jesus Christ, his only Son, our Lord,
who was born of the Virgin Mary,
was crucified, died, and was buried,
rose from the dead,
and is now seated at the right hand of the Father?

The sick person and those present reply:

I do.

The minister continues:

Do you believe in the Holy Spirit,
the holy Catholic Church, the communion of saints,
the forgiveness of sins, the resurrection of the body,
and life everlasting?

The sick person and those present reply:

I do.

Prayer for the Sick Person

If the condition of the sick person permits, a brief litany is recited by the minister in these or similar words:

My brothers and sisters, with one heart let us call on our Saviour Jesus Christ.

You loved us to the very end and gave yourself over to death in order to give us life. For our brother/sister, Lord, we pray:

The people reply:
Lord, hear our prayer.

The minister continues:
You said to us: 'All who eat my flesh and drink my blood will live for ever.' For our brother/sister, Lord, we pray:

The people reply:
Lord, hear our prayer.

The minister continues:
You invite us to join in the banquet where pain and sorrow, sadness and separation will be no more. For our brother/sister, Lord, we pray:

The people reply:
Lord, hear our prayer.

Viaticum

The minister then introduces the Lord's Prayer in these or similar words:

Now let us pray together to the Father in the words given by our Lord Jesus Christ:

He continues with all present:

Our Father, who art in heaven,
hallowed be thy name.
Thy kingdom come.
Thy will be done on earth, as it is in heaven.
Give us this day our daily bread,
and forgive us our trespasses,
as we forgive those who trespass against us,
and lead us not into temptation,
but deliver us from evil. Amen.

Then the minister shows the Holy Eucharist to those present, saying:

Behold the Lamb of God,
behold him who takes away the sins of the world.
Blessed are those called to the supper of the
Lamb.

The sick person and the other communicants say:

Lord, I am not worthy
that you should enter under my roof,
but only say the word and my soul shall be healed.

The minister goes to the sick person and, showing the Blessed Sacrament, says:

The Body of Christ (or: **The Blood of Christ**)

The sick person answers:

Amen.

The minister adds:

May the Lord Jesus Christ protect you
and lead you to eternal life.
Amen.

Others present who wish to receive communion then do so in the usual way. After the conclusion of the rite, the minister cleanses the vessel as usual. Then a period of silence may be observed. The minister says a concluding prayer. One of the following may be used.

Let us pray.

A

God of peace,
you offer eternal healing to those who believe
in you;
you have refreshed your servant N.
with food and drink from heaven:
lead him/her safely into the kingdom of light.
Through Christ our Lord.

The people reply:

Amen.

B

All-powerful and ever-living God,
may the body and blood of Christ your Son
be for our brother/sister N.
a lasting remedy for body and soul.
Through Christ our Lord.

The people reply:

Amen.

C

Father, your Son, Jesus Christ, is our way,
our truth, and our life.
Look with compassion on your servant N.
who has trusted in your promises.
You have refreshed him/her with the body
and blood of your Son:
may he/she enter your kingdom in peace.

The people reply:

Amen.

Concluding Rite

Then the minister says:

May the Lord be with you always,
to be your strength and your peace.

The minister and the others present may then give the sick person the sign of peace.